Waging Peace

A Study in Biblical Pacifism

by
John Lamoreau
and
Ralph Beebe

BARCLAY PRESS
NEWBERG, OREGON

WAGING PEACE

First Edition © 1980
Second Edition © 1981

published by
Barclay Press
Newberg, OR 97132

www.barclaypress.com

Unless otherwise noted, Scripture passages are from
the Revised Standard Version of the Bible.

ISBN: 0-913342-31-9

Printed in The United States of America

Contents

Preface

"I CAME THAT they may have life, and have it abundantly." (John 10:10)

This booklet is written for Christian pacifists who need data to support their convictions and study aids to enhance their ministry.

It is written for Christian nonpacifists who are searching for a deeper, more complete, more fulfilling dimension in their faith, but have never seriously studied Christ's call to a life of unconditional love.

It is written for non-Christians who want to make the world more loving and unselfish, but have never realized that a commitment to these purposes is the heart of Christ's message and the foundation of His kingdom on earth.

Finally, it is written for all of us who often feel powerless in our desire to do good, anticipating that we will avail ourselves of the resources of Him who said: "You shall receive power when the Holy Spirit has come upon you; and you shall be my witnesses...." (Acts 1:8)

Chapters one through three are a statement of the pacifistic message of Christ, how the early church tried to live by His teachings, and how this central message has been largely ignored and forgotten over the centuries.

The second section contains a number of scripturally based study and teaching aids designed to assist the reader in analyzing the deeper message of the Christian Gospel.

The authors are indebted to several persons who provided assistance. Arthur Roberts, Charles Beals, Ron Woodward, and Paul Mills read the manuscript and gave helpful suggestions. Dan Cadd and Gayle Beebe helped with the research; Debi Fuller and Sally Andrews assisted

5

in a variety of ways, including research and typing. Wanda Beebe checked the manuscript with a careful interpretive and editorial eye.

Finally, our thanks to Dick Eichenberger and his staff at Barclay Press, who as usual provided cooperative and efficient service.

—*John Lamoreau and Ralph Beebe*

Introduction

BIBLICAL PACIFISM rests on three foundational truths: (1) that God created and His creation is good; (2) that Christ's redemption of fallen humanity is the central point in history and opened an age when humans were empowered and expected to be witnesses of His love; and (3) that in His resurrection Christ has already won the final victory over sin.

God made man to be steward over a world with abundant resources that, if used as intended, would be ample for the earth's inhabitants. But man sinned and became exploiter and desecrater of the creation. The long-range result of this tragic fall is a world of sinful selfishness, pollution, jealousy, hatred, and war.

From the foundation of the world, however, God had a plan. "In the fullness of time" Jesus Christ, who was both human and divine, bore the weight of the world's sin in a substitutionary atonement. God's mysterious method was to sacrifice His own Son to redeem any who would accept and become His followers. Christ died that human beings might be reconciled to God and to His human and natural creation.

Redemption comes through faith— "Believe in the Lord Jesus and you will be saved" (Acts 16:31)—but Christ also expects changed behavior. "You have heard that it was said, 'You shall love your neighbor and hate your enemy," He noted. "But I say to you, Love your enemies and pray for those who persecute you." (Matthew 5:43-44) Here, indeed, was a new ethic. After His ascension, Christ's followers boldly proclaimed the same message. Paul the apostle was eloquent: "Do not be conformed to this world but be transformed by the renewal of your mind, that you may prove what is the will of God, what is good and acceptable and perfect." (Romans 12:2)

The early church was not without imperfections. Yet so devoted to Christ and His message were the Christians that for nearly 300 years they uniformly refused to fight, either for their country, in rebellion against it, or in their own self-defense. Steadfastly refusing to be conformed to this world, they lived transformed lives.[1]

Gradually, however, Christians submitted to the pressure to accommodate themselves to the world around them. The critical moment came in A.D. 312 when the Emperor Constantine accepted a watered-down version of Christianity that required no sacrifice and no obedience—one that, unbelievably, reversed Christ's teachings and made His cross the banner for military conquest. Christianity became an accepted religion and later the only legal religion in the empire. Having once been persecuted, Christians became the persecutors; whereas before A.D. 173 no Christians were in the army, by A.D. 417 the Roman military would accept only Christians.[2]

This development severely blunted the forward thrust of Christianity. The testimony that "we must obey God rather than men" (Acts 5:29) gave way to the belief that killing was justifiable if done by the state's military to protect its citizens' interests. Years later, in the me-

---

[1] Roland H. Bainton, *Christian Attitudes Toward War and Peace* (Nashville: Abingdon, 1960), pp. 66-84; Alan Kreider and John H. Yoder, "Christians and War," in Eerdmans' *Handbook to the History of Christianity* (Grand Rapids: Eerdmans, 1977), p. 25; Kenneth Scott Latourette, *A History of Christianity* (New York: Harper & Brothers, 1953), p. 242; Paul Ramsey, *War and the Christian Conscience* (Durham: Duke University Press, 1961), p. xv; Guy Franklin Hershberger, *War, Peace, and Nonresistance* (Scottdale, Pa.: Herald Press, 1953), pp. 65-70; C. J. Cadoux, *The Early Christian Attitude to War* (London: George Alien & Unwin, Ltd., 1917), p. 17.

[2] Bainton, p. 88.

dieval crusades, an apostate church led European nations into "holy war" against the infidel. "Our men rode in the blood of the Saracens up to the knees of the horses," triumphantly proclaimed one follower of the cross and the flag.[3]

Even today, many Christians feel killing is justified under some circumstances. Yet there is a corresponding resurgence of concern that Christians return to the ethic provided by Christ—that of living out in the world His message of love and peace.

What, then, of the future? Christians know the joyous end of the story—an eternity of peace with Jesus, who has already won the victory over sin and death. But meanwhile, many feel a deep commitment to try to live as Christ taught, making His kingdom on earth a foretaste of heaven. They feel compelled to be leaven to the world around, calling other Christians to be accountable to Christ.

This booklet is dedicated to helping Christ's church regain a vision of its true message—that of love and peace, as He commanded His followers. It is hoped that this work might assist Christians to be evangelists for Christ, witnesses of the power of Pentecost, which He promised would be the mark of His disciples—the power to love each other, to be good stewards of His creation, and to wage peace in His name. *That* Christ, if truly lifted up, will draw all men unto Him.

---

[3] Daimbert, Archbishop of Pisa, 1099, quoted in Stanley I. Stuber, *How We Got Our Denominations* (New York: Association Press, 1951), p. 95.

What Christ Teaches about Violence

JESUS TAUGHT PEACE to a world filled with violence. During the six centuries preceding His birth, Jerusalem, the Holy City, was under the almost constant rule of foreign tyrants. Under rulers such as Nebuchadnezzar (586 B.C.), Alexander the Great (332 B.C.), Antiochus Epiphanes (175 B.C.), and Herod the Idumean (37 B.C.), Jerusalem became a prize to the world's mightiest armies. It was into the latter part of Herod's reign that Jesus was born.

The Jews eagerly awaited the coming Messiah. For centuries they had been mistreated, abused, and scorned. The Christ, they thought, would bring a new day of national honor and patriotic pride. He would come in glory and honor as a military leader who would break ungodly nations "with a rod of iron" and "dash them in pieces like a potter's vessel." (Psalm 2:9)

Any nation that would not serve Him would perish. He would establish peace by crushing the enemy. Persecution of the Jews would stop; sons of the persecutors would bow at their feet; kings would minister to them; foreigners would build their walls and tend their flocks (Isaiah 60:10-14; 61:5). No longer would their grain be given as food to their enemies or foreigners drink their new wine (Isaiah 62:8-9). Instead of humiliation they would shout for joy over their double portion. When the conquering Messiah came they would feed on the wealth of nations and array themselves in magnificence (Isaiah 61:6-7). Weeping would cease; infant mortality would vanish; anyone who lived but one hundred years would be thought accursed (Isaiah 65:19-22). Such were the messianic expectations of the Jews.

Then Jesus came. But he came as a humble servant, not as a military leader. From His birth in a manger to His training as a carpenter His life confused the Jews. It is true that some prophecies indicated He might come as a suffering servant, but after centuries of forced suffering few were open to this possibility. His ministry seems to have been a complete surprise and a disappointment to many.

Jesus' teaching and example were the very antithesis of their hopes and expectations. What they had expected to be accomplished He did in a fuller measure, but through nonviolence. He taught them to go an extra mile—voluntarily—for their enemies who legally forced them to go one (Matthew 5:41). He commanded them to do good to those who hated them, to pray for those who mistreated them, to love those they had the most reason to hate (Luke 6:27, 28, 35). All these things were required of them if they were to be sons of God (Matthew 5:44-45).

Instead of removing the shackles of persecution in favor of the worldly peace they anticipated, Jesus told them that as believers the persecutions would actually increase. At a time when they thought they were to gain the power to take revenge on their oppressors, He told them to turn the other cheek and not resist the evil done to them (Matthew 5:39). If they chose to be His disciples, He warned, they would be struck, arrested, flogged, cursed, hated, mistreated, ostracized, betrayed, insulted, and killed (Matthew 10:22-23, 28; Mark 13:9, 11, 12; Luke 6:22, 28; Luke 21:12-17; John 15:20). And when these things happened He told them not to resist but to leap for joy (Luke 6:23). Further, He taught them that even hateful anger was evil—as much so as murder—and that they were not to harbor contempt in their hearts (Matthew 5:22).

"Love the Lord your God with all your heart, and with all your soul, and with all your mind...[and] your neighbor as yourself." (Matthew 22:37-39; Luke 10:27-28) These two greatest commandments summed up all the laws and were familiar to the Jews. But Jesus shocked and angered them by declaring that even the despised Samaritans were their neighbors (Luke 10:29-37).

How difficult it must have been for the Jews to accept Jesus as the almighty King when He would let himself be crowned with thorns, beaten, and crucified, without resisting, and not even allow himself to be defended! How hard it must have been to follow a liberator who proclaimed a lifestyle of increased servitude and suffering!

Unfortunately, His behavior and teachings were too difficult for many of the Jews. They could not accept the Prince of Peace. And they missed their salvation.

Yet had Jesus chosen, He could have been the military Messiah His people anticipated. Satan offered Him all the world's kingdoms with all their splendor, if only He would bow down and worship him (Matthew 4:8-9; Luke 4:5-7). Jesus then and there could have become the king of the Roman Empire and dictator of the world. As the worldly king He could have "freed" the Jews and all oppressed people. But He said *no*! His kingdom was not of this world (John 18:36). When Jesus spoke, multitudes listened. He could have led them in a vengeance-filled armed attack. But He said *no*. And irony of ironies—he told them they were actually blessed in their downtrodden state (Matthew 5:10-12)!

Jesus' teachings were exemplified in His everyday behavior. A centurion of the Roman army once came asking Jesus to heal his servant (Matthew 8:5-13). Jesus gladly offered His assistance and sought to go immediately to the sick servant, but the centurion thought Jesus could perform the healing from where He stood. Amazed, Jesus stated that He had not found such faith in Israel. He then healed the servant.

What had Jesus done? A Roman soldier had come asking for help. Jesus knew that the Romans were oppressors in the land of Israel. He knew it was soldiers who murdered the infants at Bethlehem. He knew they worshiped Caesar as a false god. He knew of the sexual immorality in the Roman state. And He knew the Roman soldiers would soon mock, flog, and crucify Him. But this Christ, who had taught His followers to go an extra mile for the Romans, who had taught them to love the enemy and to do good to them, displayed a love that transcended vindictiveness. He healed the Roman servant.

Jesus' priorities are astounding. He taught peace— yet He was facing a man of war. He was God—yet this was a man who, as a Roman soldier, worshiped Caesar as God. But Jesus loved unconditionally. He knew His act of love must precede the centurion's salvation and potential change of behavior. He was simply, and beautifully, loving and helping one who was His assumed enemy, just as He had taught others to do.

Another example of Jesus' method occurred shortly before His arrest (Luke 22:36-51). Here He instructed His disciples to sell their robes and buy swords if they had none. His disciples, misunderstanding His metaphor, replied that they had two. He told them that was enough. Two swords! Enough to fight the entire Roman legion?

They proceeded to the Mount of Olives and Jesus knelt and prayed that if the Father was willing, the cup (of crucifixion) might be removed from Him, but added that it was His Father's will that must be done. An angel then appeared to strengthen Him. He was in agony and praying fervently; His sweat became like drops of blood and fell to the ground. He arose from His prayer and found the disciples sleeping. He awakened them and told them to pray that they might not enter into temptation. While He was speaking a contingent of Roman soldiers led by Judas approached. The disciples realized what was about to happen and asked: "Lord, shall we strike with the sword?" (Luke 22:49) Without awaiting a reply, one of them took a swing at the slave of the high priest and cut off his right ear. Jesus ordered his defenders to stop. He then healed the injured servant.

What had happened? Jesus' crucifixion was near. He asked that this cup might be removed. He was in agony as He prayed. The soldiers came. He knew inhuman torture would soon follow. A disciple tried to protect Him and in doing so injured one of the group that came to arrest Him. Jesus rebuked him. And then He healed the man! Jesus was in agony over what was about to happen, yet He still found time to heal the injured servant! Love your enemies, He taught. Do good to them, He preached, even in a time of persecution. And at the critical moment, that was exactly what Jesus did.

The centurion and the injured man—both were supposed enemies. But Jesus touched them in love. A soldier and a servant—perhaps both were at the crucifixion. Yet instead of hating the gentle man on the cross, they must have felt sorrow and compassion and a willingness to respond to His teaching and example. We do not know if they became Christians, but we do know He gave them another chance based on love acted out in kindness. Their potential for response was surely increased a thousandfold by His unconditional love.

15

Jesus again witnessed to His gospel of love and peace at the crucifixion. After He was nailed to the cross He said: "Father, forgive them; for they know not what they do." (Luke 23:34) In the pain, the torment, the agony, the embarrassment of crucifixion, Jesus lived out His life as He taught others to live theirs—in unconditional love.

As glorious as this is, the story does not end there. Through the gift of salvation, Christ offered to His disciples and the world the ability to live in His love. "By this shall men know that you are my disciples, that you love one another." (John 13:35) In the power of Pentecost, the disciples lived in that love.

The disciples were tortured. They were beaten. They were executed. Yet they loved even their attackers. "Lord, do not hold this sin against them," Stephen prayed as he was being stoned to death (Acts 7:60). Why? Because he understood the will of God and the importance of the gift of eternal life. He wanted others to share with him in that gift—even if they were his attackers.

"Lord, do not hold this sin against them." He could pray nothing else. His desire was to be an instrument of love leading them to salvation. He did not want to be a cause of their damnation. He had no other choice but to pray for his attackers. He was simply doing as Jesus had taught, following the Lord's example and letting the Holy Spirit control his life.

What if the disciples had disobeyed Christ's teaching and taken the sword to try to free Stephen? Their testimony would have been destroyed. Further, the situation presents an astounding possibility: suppose Saul of Tarsus, who was standing nearby, had been attacked by the Christians. Would he have ever seen the light on the road

16

to Damascus? Suppose Peter and Paul had killed each other in the struggle!

Another clear witness to the apostles' nonviolence is given by Paul and Silas (Acts 16:19-29). They had been arrested for commanding a spirit of divination to come out of a slave girl, resulting in a loss of income for her owners. As a result they were brought before the authorities, beaten, and thrown into prison. For doing good they were fastened in stocks and forced to sit in what was very likely a cold, damp, rat-infested cell.

How did Paul and Silas respond? They prayed! They sang hymns of praise to God and witnessed to the other prisoners! And when an earthquake freed them and they saw the jailer about to kill himself in fear that the prisoners had escaped, Paul called out to him, stopped the suicide, and convinced the jailer of the love of Christ. The jailer was saved, and so was his family.

Paul and Silas could have let the jailer kill himself and they probably would have escaped. In revealing themselves they risked being shackled again, and perhaps punished. But that wasn't important. What was important was that an unsaved man was about to commit suicide and condemn himself to damnation. They had a chance to reach out to him in love and lead him into salvation. In Christ they had no choice. They had to love the person who participated in their torture, even if it meant more suffering for them. This was Christ's example. This was what Christ had taught. This had to be their example also.

Peace is central to the teaching of Jesus and the apostles. To comprehend the full meaning of "love your neighbor as yourself" is to understand what the meaning of peace really is.

The lifestyles of the apostles are truly amazing in the depth of their love for all people, whether friend or foe. Jesus states:

If you love those who love you, what credit is that to you? For even sinners love those who love them. And if you do good to those who do good to you, what credit is that to you? For even sinners do the same. And if you lend to those from whom you hope to receive, what credit is that to you? Even sinners lend to sinners, to receive as much again. But love your enemies, and do good, and lend, expecting nothing in return; and your reward will be great, and you will be sons of the Most High; for he is kind to the ungrateful and the selfish. Be merciful, even as your Father is merciful. Judge not and you will not be judged; condemn not, and you will not be condemned; forgive, and you will be forgiven (Luke 6:32-37).

Jesus said this not only to the Twelve but also to the masses coming to Him. The early Christians believed what He said. They taught it. They lived it. And, in the power of Pentecost, His followers are expected to live it today.

What the Christian Church Has Taught about Violence

THE CHRISTIAN CHURCH followed Christ's teaching of nonviolence for nearly 300 years. Then it entered a long, dark age of support for nationalistic wars from which it has not yet emerged. Although through the years a remnant of believers has tried to live by His non-violent example, the Church since A.D. 300 has generally strayed far from the pacifistic demands of His Gospel.

Christ said, "Love your enemies." Paul added, "Overcome evil with good." It is clear that Christians in the postbiblical age continued to live and teach this message. So universal was this affirmation that every Christian statement on the subject dating from the first 300 years that survives today opposes Christian participation in war. There are no exceptions. There is no record of any early Christian having written anything that condoned war.[1]

Here is a sampling of the many early writings in which Christians stated their opposition to bloodshed.[2]

Tertullian (150-225): "Christ in disarming Peter ungirt every soldier....Shall the son of peace, for whom it is unlawful to go to war, be engaged in battle?"

Justin Martyr (c. 165): "We who were filled with war and mutual slaughter and every wickedness have each of us in all the world changed our weapons of

---

[1] Kenneth Scott Latourette, *A History of Christianity* (New York: Harper & Brothers, 1953), p. 242. See also the other references in Introduction.

[2] These are all quoted from Bainton, pp. 66-84. For numerous additional examples see also Richard McSorley, S. J., *New Testament Basis of Peacemaking* (Washington, D.C.: Center for Peace Studies, 1979), pp. 71-90; also see Arthur F. Holmes, *War and Christian Ethics* (Grand Rapids: Baker Book House, 1975).

war—swords into plows and spears into agricultural instruments. We who formerly murdered one another now not only do not make war upon our enemies but gladly die confessing Christ."

Lactantius (c. 304); "It can never be lawful for a righteous man to go to war."

Clement (c. 200); "If you enroll as one of God's people, heaven is your country and God your lawgiver. What then are his laws? 'Thou shalt not kill. Thou shalt love thy neighbor as thyself. To him that strikes thee on the one cheek turn also the other.'"

It is clear that these early Christians believed it was totally inconsistent to be a Christian and go to war. From the world's point of view the Christians were completely impractical, even insane. For example, when one 21-year-old Christian, Maximilianus (c. 295) was commanded to enlist in the Roman army, he replied: "I cannot serve as a soldier. I cannot do evil. I am a Christian." Like Stephen, James, and other earlier apostles, he was executed.[3]

Marcellus, a centurion, became a Christian. He refused to fight, so was thrown into prison, but said "I threw down [my arms]; for it was not seemly that a Christian man, who renders military service to the Lord Christ, should render it [also] by [inflicting] earthly injuries." They killed him, but the clerk of the court was so impressed he accepted Christ and was also executed.[4] So, even though Christian obedience was not practical from the human perspective, anything less would violate God's higher law and therefore be totally impractical from the Christian viewpoint.

Because they would render to Caesar only what was Caesar's, Christians were considered unpatriotic and disloyal. In a famous attack on them, Celsus complained that

---

[3] Quoted in Cadoux, p. 149. See also J. C. Wenges, *The Way of Peace* (Scottdale, Pa.: Herald Press, 1977), p. 16; McSorley, pp. 83-86.

[4] Quoted in Cadoux, p. 152.

if all the citizens of the empire were pacifists like the Christians, the empire would fall victim to barbarians. One leader, Origen (185-254), admitted that the Christians were pacifists, but predicted that if all Romans were to become Christians, and therefore pacifists, the barbarians would too. The Christian minority, he argued, was already doing more with its love, labor, and prayers to preserve the empire than all the Roman armies.[5]

The first record of any Christian having served in the military is in 173.[6] Gradually more Christians joined, but even by 300 the majority of Christians still were refusing to serve. Roland Bainton, professor of ecclesiastical history at Yale Divinity School, calls the first three centuries "the age of pacifism." Allan Kreider and John Howard Yoder note: "The Christian church of the first three centuries was pacifist. The early Christians combined a simple obedience to the words of Jesus with a genuine international spirit." Historians of this period uniformly agree with these conclusions.[7]

Although it is likely that by the end of the third century most Christians still clung to their pacifism, it also is clear that many were beginning to accommodate themselves to the Roman state and were entering the army. A tragic change was occurring. Its crux came in 312 when Constantine, the emperor of Rome, reported that he sought the help of the Christian God in battle and saw a vision of the cross with the words "conquer by this." He

---

[5] Latourette, p. 243.

[6] Bainton, p. 68.

[7] As noted earlier the standard sources are Latourette, Bainton, Ramsey, Cadoux, and the Kreider and Yoder article. Although some historians are silent on this issue, the authors have found none who refute the position taken here.

won the battle and eventually decided to become a Christian and make Christianity an accepted religion.[8]

Roland Bainton reports that the religion of one God and the empire of one ruler came to be seen by Roman officials as having been made for each other. Polytheism had been a religion appropriate for a multiplicity of city-states perpetually in strife, "but monotheism and universal monarchy were congruous, and to the confession of one faith, one lord, and one baptism could now be added that of one empire and one emperor."[9] Christianity soon became the only officially sanctioned religion.

Christians had gained a vested interest in the empire; no longer could they speak out clearly in moral judgment about war, for as the empire began to collapse, their privileged position was endangered, and many responded to the call for national defense. Christianity had been co-opted into the service of the nation and thus entered a new phase that would have been anathema to the earlier followers of Christ.

Augustine, bishop of Hippo, was an apologist for this change. He rationalized it by describing dual tracks—the city of God and the city of man. Human beings live in a sinful world and therefore most have to fight: "Do not think that it is impossible for anyone to please God while engaged in active military service. Among such persons was the holy David, to whom God gave so great a testimony; among them also were many righteous men of that time." War, said Augustine, must not be fought if a just cause did not exist. It could not be engaged in for unrighteous, aggressive, or selfish reasons. But "when war is

---

[8] Richard A. Todd, "Constantine and the Christian Empire," in Eerdmans' *Handbook to the History of Christianity* (Grand Rapids: Eerdmans, 1977), pp. 130-131. This story varies slightly from source to source, but there is general agreement as to the essentials.

[9] Bainton, p. 87.

undertaken in obedience to God, who would rebuke, or humble, or crush the pride of man, it must be allowed to be a righteous war."[10]

So, the just war theory became a part of Christianity. The church began to see itself on the level of Old Testament Israel, and renounced the peaceful message of Christ in favor of killing in the defense of a nation they hoped He would honor. Soon every war was considered justifiable and worthy of God's blessing. The Roman empire disintegrated; new nations were formed, each considering itself God's favorite. Each struggled for the blessing of the church as Christians killed Christians across national boundaries.

In 1095 Pope Urban II, hoping to unite Christendom in a war against the Moslems, called for a great crusade:[11]

We have heard, most beloved brethren, and you heard what we cannot recount without deep sorrow—how with great hurt and dire sufferings, our Christian brothers, members in Christ, are scourged, oppressed and injured in Jerusalem....Christian blood, redeemed by the blood of Christ, has been shed, and Christian flesh, akin to the flesh of Christ, has been subjected to unspeakable degradation.... [by the] base and bastard Turks....

...You will go forth, through the gift of God and the privilege of St. Peter, absolved from all your sins ....They who die will enter the mansion of heaven....

It is, in truth, [God's] will! And let these words be your war-cry when you unsheath your swords against the enemy. You are soldiers of the cross: wear, then, on your breast or your shoulders the blood red sign of Him who died for the salvation of your souls. Wear it as a token that his help will never fail you: wear it as a pledge of a vow which can never be recalled.

---

[10] Augustine to Count Boniface, quoted in Holmes, pp. 61, 62, 65.
[11] Quoted in Stuber, pp. 93-94.

23

One half century later Bernard of Clairvaux urged a second crusade.[12]

The earth is shaken because the Lord of Heaven is losing his land, the land in which he appeared to men, in which he lived amongst men for more than thirty years; the land made glorious by his miracles, holy by his blood....Gird yourself therefore like men and take up arms with joy and with zeal for your Christian name, in order to take vengeance on the heathen....O mighty soldiers, O men of war, you have a cause for which you can fight without danger to your souls; a cause in which to conquer is glorious and for which to die is gain.

...Take up the sign of the Cross and you will find indulgence for all the sins which you humbly confess....

It is an act of Christian piety to vanquish the proud....

Those Christians who were taking up arms in Christ's name probably were not really familiar with His teachings. It is unlikely that many of the crusaders understood that Christ commanded His followers to love their enemies. The Gospel had become locked in the Mass and church tradition. To a considerable extent the loving Christ of Calvary had been replaced with a vengeful Christ who was misrepresented as an advocate of nationalism and war.

Then, over the course of several centuries, reform began to take place. Martin Luther and many others led the way to a revival of Christian faith. Justification was recognized as being by faith, and human beings were seen as bearing responsibility for their own salvation through a relationship with God. The door was open, it would seem, for a return to the full vitality of Christ's message.

---

[12] Bernard of Clairvaux, quoted in Holmes, pp. 88, 90, 91.

Sadly, though, the Reformation proved to be incomplete. While Luther and the others sought Christ with deep devotion, they seem not to have grasped the full significance of Christ's message of love, which had ushered in a new kingdom based upon nonvindictiveness. Through his influence Luther furthered and popularized Augustine's "two kingdom" theory with its conflicting loyalties. In his relationships with warlike opponents, he seems to have been more greatly influenced by the Old Testament and church tradition than by the teachings of Christ and the example of early Christians. He was a product of the medieval feudal system, believing it was proper for those in authority to go to war to suppress rebellion, although it was not acceptable for wars to be fought against those in political authority. To him, killing was justifiable for the maintenance of peace, to punish wrongdoers, and to keep peasants obedient. His defense of violence in a righteous cause includes this confusing argument:[13]

The hand that wields this sword and kills with it is not man's hand, but God's; and it is not man, but God, who hangs, tortures, beheads, kills, and fights. All of these are God's works and judgments....

If we...admitted that war was wrong in itself, then we'd have to give in on all other points and allow that the use of the sword was entirely wrong. For if it is wrong to use a sword in war, it is also wrong to use a sword to punish evil doers or to keep peace....

...Christ teaches us not to resist evil but rather to suffer all things (Matthew 5:39-42).... Indeed, Christians do not fight and have no worldly rulers among them. Their government is a spiritual government, and, according to the Spirit, they are subjects of no one but Christ. Nevertheless, as far as body and property are concerned they are subject to worldly rulers and owe them obedience. If worldly rulers call

---

[13]Martin Luther, quoted in Holmes, pp. 143, 145, 146.

upon them to fight, then they ought to and must fight and be obedient, not as Christians, but as members of the state and obedient subjects....

That most reformed Christians failed to live according to Christ's commandment to love the enemy is further seen in this statement by Oliver Cromwell, whose Puritan armies killed thousands of Catholics: "I am persuaded that this is a righteous judgment of God upon these barbarous wretches...."[14] Each member of Cromwell's army carried a "Soldier's Pocket Bible," in which were combined three verses from the Sermon on the Mount, Chronicles, and Psalms that read: "But I say unto you, Love your enemies. Wouldst thou help the wicked and love them that hate the Lord? Do not I hate them, O Lord, that hate thee?...I hate them with an unfeigned hatred as they were mine utter enemies." (Matthew 5:44; 2 Chronicles 19:2; Psalm 139:21, 22) The summary states that the soldier must "Love his enemies as they are his enemies, and hate them as they are God's enemies." Cromwell's armies revived an old crusading text: "Cursed be he that keeps back his hand from shedding blood."[15]

Meanwhile, Puritans in America were thanking God for sending smallpox, which killed hundreds of Indians and made it easier for the Christians to take possession of the new world.[16] Later, when more Indians were in the way and "God" failed to provide another smallpox epidemic, the Puritans did the killing themselves.[17]

To the Puritans, God was commander in holy wars against Roman Catholics, the Church of England, Indians,

---

[14] Quoted in Bainton, p. 151.

[15] Quoted in Bainton, p. 150.

[16] From *New England's First Fruits* (London, 1643), p. 36, quoted in Alden T. Vaughan, ed., *The Puritan Tradition in America*, 1620-1730 (Columbia, S.C.; University of South Carolina Press, 1972), p. 65.

[17] *Ibid.*, p. 66.

Quakers, and infidels. They saw themselves as chosen people crusading against the ungodly. But they were not alone. Other Protestant denominations and many Catholics also invoked God's name in the conquest of the new world. Later, individuals such as Nat Turner and John Brown were to report that God commanded them to kill people in attempts to incite slave rebellions.[18] Behavior based upon belief that God leads righteous people to kill the unrighteous has been repeated over and over again in many countries.

In recent centuries Christians have also often been involved in defending secular nations against their enemies. The statement of United States naval commander Stephen Decatur in the War of 1812 perhaps comes close to the position of many modern Christians: "Our country: in her intercourse with foreign nations may she always be in the right; but our country, right or wrong."[19]

World War I provides an example. Kaiser Wilhelm explained Germany's entrance into the war by saying: "We are inspired by the unalterable will to protect the place which God has set for ourselves and all coming generations....In a defensive war that has been forced upon us, with a clear conscience and a clean hand, we take up the sword." The Kaiser's Imperial Chancellor added: "Only in defense of a just cause shall our sword fly from its scabbard."[20]

Yet Americans killing these Germans were calling for a crusade against what they saw as the "demonic Hun"; the Young Men's Christian Association was producing

---

[18] Quoted in Alien Weinstein and R. Jackson Wilson, *Freedom and Crisis* (New York: Random House, 1974), pp. 281 and 362.

[19] Stephen Decatur, April 1816, quoted in Burton Stephenson, ed., *The Home Book of Quotations* (New York: Dodd, Mead and Company, 1949), p. 63.

[20] Hanna Hafkesbrink, *Unknown Germany* (New Haven: Yale University Press, 1948), pp. 76-77.

literature calling for Christianizing "every phase of a righteous war." In the words of its secretary: "I would not enter this work until I could see Jesus Himself...running a bayonet through an enemy's body."[21] Banners in patriotic parades announced: "Hell is too good for the Hun."

American involvement in World War I did go beyond a simplistic "our country right or wrong" stance, however. It was also a manifestation of what might be termed a "neo-just war" position,[22] which taught that the nation's mission was fulfilled in protecting countries that could not protect themselves. President Wilson's announcement that the purpose was to keep the world safe for democracy was an extension of an earlier avowal that it was this country's special mission—her manifest destiny—to take possession of all the continent with God's blessing, and make it a bastion of freedom throughout the world. By the turn of the century this idealism had contributed much to the belief that the United States could lead the way to a peaceful world. Thus, many accepted a visionary pacifism based upon a combination of progressive idealism, American nationalism, and the social gospel. But for many the veneer of pacifism slid away and revealed an underlying advocacy of the just war when in 1917 they perceived that the ultimate goal of a peaceful world could best be served by involvement in a temporary "war to end all wars."

In recent decades the United States has engaged in more "neo-just wars" to stop fascism and communism. While both sides in these wars ignore Christ's teachings and none, even World War II, come close to meeting the requirements for a just war as laid down by Augustine, many Christians condone the killing as necessary for the

---

[21] Quoted in Martin Marty, "Time Ripe for Another Military Crusade," *Oregonian*, April 21, 1980.

[22] Inis L. Claude, Jr., "Just Wars: Doctrines and Institutions," *Political Science Quarterly*, Spring, 1980, pp. 83-96.

good of their own nation and those it defends, and therefore feel it is justifiable. Such wars are fought to preserve freedom, including religious freedom, thus creating the irony of a people disobeying Christ in order to protect their right to worship Him and spread His message.

The church continues today to contribute to a strong anti-Communist hysteria that produces so much fear that a "first-strike" capability is often advocated as necessary for deterrence. The clear message is that the United States must remain number one militarily.

When about 200,000 Christians engaged in a "Washington for Jesus" rally at the nation's capital in 1980, the call for national repentance included repentance for the nation's perceived military weakness. One of America's greatest problems is that it is "outgunned" by the Russians, Pat Robertson lamented. His cochairman, Bill Bright, agreed that if the United States becomes better armed "our enemies will not threaten us."[23]

Yet there has been a corresponding resurgence of concern about the use of armaments for Christian purposes. A serious reappraisal is being made by some leaders who now believe that in a nuclear age no war can be just.

Billy Graham, in stating his newly developed conviction that all nuclear weapons should be eliminated and that "Mr. Truman made a mistake in dropping the first atomic bomb," noted recently: "I think there's a vast change taking place in the [evangelical] community. I don't think they were aware of the potential horror of what a nuclear war with present weapons could do to the human race. And I think that they're awakening to the fact that they have a responsibility to speak out.... I didn't really

[23] Phil M. Shenk, "Washington for Jesus," *Sojourners* (June, 1980), p. 11. See also Edward E. Plowman, "Washington for Jesus: Revival Fervor and Political Proclaimer," *Christianity Today* (May 23, 1980), pp. 46-47.

give it the thought that I should have given it in my earlier years. But I've come to the conviction that this is the teaching of the Bible."[24]

Graham's position is supported by Jimmy Allen, president of the Southern Baptist Convention. In explaining the SBC's resolution in 1979 that called for multilateral nuclear disarmament, Allen said: "We are playing out scenarios of destruction for humanity. And in the midst of that kind of stockpiling and potential we have a responsibility of Christ—as Christians—to talk in terms of what you do to deal with that kind of problem in human experience."[25]

The growing list of what might be termed "nuclear pacifists" includes John R. W. Stott, rector emeritus of All Souls Church in London, who condemns nuclear war as "ethically indefensible." He says, "Although not until Christ returns will all 'swords be beaten into plowshares and spears into pruninghooks...' this fact cannot be made an excuse for building sword and spear factories. God himself is a peacemaker. If we want to qualify as his authentic children, we must be peacemakers, too."[26]

Lewis B. Schmedes, professor at Fuller Theological Seminary and a just war advocate, now believes that "no all-out nuclear war can ever be a just war, and...no provocation by any nation can justify our beginning one."[27] Arthur F. Holmes of Wheaton College agrees: "I cannot see how a world war with modern weaponry could ever again be justified."[28]

---

[24] Billy Graham, from transcript of *CBS Evening News with Walter Cronkite,* telecast March 29, 1979, in "Billy Graham Drops the Bomb," *Christianity and Crisis,* April 3, 1979, p. 111.

[25] *Ibid;* See also *Christian Century,* March 14, 1979, pp. 268-269.

[26] John R. W. Stott, "Calling for Peacemakers in a Nuclear Age, Part I," *Christianity Today,* February 8, 1980, p. 45.

[27] Lewis B. Schmedes, in *Eternity,* June 1980, p. 15.

[28] Arthur F. Holmes, *Ibid.,* p. 16.

Most of these "nuclear pacifists" still believe a limited "conventional" war might under some circumstances be justifiable. Others are beginning to speak out in disagreement. The continuing voice of the historic peace churches (Mennonite, Friends, Brethren) is now being joined by many who are taking a harder look at the ethical implications of the Gospel. Some who became disillusioned with the war in Vietnam have begun to raise significant questions about all war. Underlying their position is a call for a return to a biblical faith and acceptance of the deeper message of Christ.

Jim Wallis, editor of *Sojourners,* is a foremost spokesman: "Jesus told us to love our enemies. Reviving our capacity to love has become an urgent political necessity as the superpowers come to regard millions of their neighbors as nothing more than expendable populations in a nuclear exchange. We face unimaginable destruction unless our hearts are enlarged to recognize a neighbor in the face of our enemy."[29]

Ronald J. Sider, a professor at Eastern Baptist Theological Seminary, is persuaded that it will require a thoroughly biblical (and therefore nonviolent) faith to answer the injustice in the world. As the Christian "challenges the oppressor with a gentle firmness that underlies God's love for him, the evangelical practitioner of nonviolence can invite the oppressor to repent and change even while opposing his evil actions....If God in Christ reconciled his enemies by suffering servanthood, then those who want to follow Christ faithfully dare not treat their enemies in any other way." Sider also declares: "Christians do not claim that we should wait to live by the kingdom's standards on lying, theft, or adultery until non-Christians stop lying, stealing, and fornicating. Nor should

---

[29] Jim Wallis, *Ibid.,* p. 18.

the church delay implementing Jesus' nonviolent method of overcoming evil with good until the Caesars and Hitlers disappear."[30]

Even some of those who might be tempted by the "zealot option" of combating oppression with violence have spoken out for peaceful methods. Martin Luther King, whose nonviolent direct action is well known, asserted that "we will never be true sons of our heavenly Father until we love our enemies and pray for those who persecute us." Because "returning hate for hate multiplies hate, we must find in Christ the strength to love."[31]

John Perkins, founder of Voice of Calvary Ministries in Mississippi, is developing a "quiet revolution" through the church to bring hope to those whose lives have been severely damaged by racism. In a chapter entitled "Why I Can't Hate Anymore," Perkins recalls that while being severely beaten he could only pity the oppressor for what the disease of racism had done. He adds:

Some of my [fellow black] people were saying, "Fight back! Use violence! Arm for the revolution...."

I saw how my bitterness could destroy me. The Spirit of God had a hold of me and wouldn't let me sidestep his justice. And his justice said that I was just as sinful as those who beat me. But I knew that God's justice is seasoned with forgiveness. Forgiveness is what makes his justice redemptive. Forgiveness! That was the key. And somehow, God's forgiveness for me was tied up in my forgiveness of those who hurt me. In the hospital room I would reread Matthew 6 over and over, especially where Jesus says, "For if you forgive men their trespasses, your heavenly Father will also forgive you; but if you

---

[30] Ronald J. Sider, in Maynard Shelly, *New Call for Peacemakers* (Newton, Kans.: Faith and Life Press, 1979), pp. 38, 46, 48. See also Ronald J. Sider, *Christ and Violence* (Scottdale, Pa.: Herald Press, 1979).

[31] Martin Luther King, Jr., *Strength to Love* (New York: Pocket Books, Inc., 1964), pp. 45, 50.

do not forgive men their trespasses, neither will your Father forgive your trespasses." (Matthew 6:14-15)[32]

Forgiveness is the key, John Perkins says. It is encouraging that today so many are learning to seek and extend forgiveness. Total peace is not possible this side of heaven, but the redeemed Christian living a life of forgiving love already has the peace only Christ can give. It is noteworthy that the current revival of interest in serious biblical study and commitment to Christ's teachings makes an increased acceptance of pacifism inevitable.

---

[32] John Perkins, *A Quiet Revolution* (Waco, Texas: Word Books, Publisher, 1976), p. 191.

Unconditional Love

"BLESSED ARE THE PEACEMAKERS, for they shall be called sons of God." (Matthew 5:9)

Jesus taught and practiced unconditional love for all people. In doing so He called His followers to a higher standard than that of sinners, who loved only those who did good to them. He desired that Christians be a reflection of His love as He was a reflection of His Father's love (John 15:9-12). Paul wrote that this love is "patient and kind...is not arrogant or rude...does not insist on its own way...endures all things." (1 Corinthians 13) This is the love that leads to a life of nonviolence.

There is no biblical record of any Christian who did not believe in this ethic. Paul, Peter, James, John, Silas, Stephen—these were all men whom the Holy Spirit taught and controlled. They lived in a world filled with violence, and they responded with love. They were pacifists. They cared. They were active. They got involved. They were continually risking their lives not only for their friends but for their enemies as well. They left a marvelous example for all to follow. To these early Christians, pacifism was not an option but an essential and natural result of following Christ.

The apostle John writes that "any one who hates his brother is a murderer; and you know that no murderer has eternal life abiding in him." (1 John 3:15) Paul adds that people who practice such things as strife, jealousy, anger, and envy shall not inherit the kingdom of God (Galatians 5:19-21). Jesus warned that even to have contempt for others makes one "liable to the hell of fire." (Matthew 5:22) He told the church in Ephesus that unless they returned to the heights of their "first love" their salvation would be in jeopardy (Revelation 2:1-5).

Christians today face the challenge to align their practices with the teachings of the One whose name they bear. While admitting that a world of total peace is not possible this side of heaven, many are grieved that the cross of Christ has so often been made the symbol of conquest. They call for a renewed study of, and dedication to, the teachings of Christ. The result will be a marvelous spiritual revival.

To the Christians who will one day face the attack of the "beast" and his armies Jesus warned that if anyone kills with the sword, with the sword he must be killed. He then added: "Here is a call for the endurance and faith of the saints." (Revelation 13:10) Jesus further stated He will come with "a sharp sword" with which He will slay those who have not followed His will (Revelation 19).

Jesus stated: "He who rejects me and does not receive my sayings has a judge; the word that I have spoken will be his judge on the last day." (John 12:48) Both the word that judges and the sword that slays come from the mouth of Jesus.

"Judge not, and you will not be judged; condemn not and you will not be condemned; forgive and you will be forgiven." (Luke 6:37) Whenever we kill, for whatever reason, we become the judge, jury, and executioner. The implications are clear: If we judge we shall be judged. If we condemn we shall be condemned. If we fail to pardon we shall not be granted pardon.

It is perhaps not surprising that the modern Christian church is so largely nonpacifistic. Christ's teachings seem difficult to follow. Perhaps even more importantly, the example of the early church has been mostly forgotten. Few Christians today are aware of any norm except that which has been followed since Constantine. Many

Christians fail to give Christ's "love-your-enemies" ethic serious consideration.

Most Christian nations are depicted at least to some degree as modern versions of Old Testament Israel. This is perhaps most true of the United States, which is seen as especially gifted and as God's chosen nation for spreading His message. "Go into all the world and preach the gospel" (Mark 16:15), Christ said. The United States, more than any other modern nation, has responded to this commandment. Does it not follow that the nation that is thus central to missionary efforts should be kept strong? Is it not justifiable to use force to keep open the doors for evangelism?

Further, many see Christ's message as weak and therefore impractical. It challenges the norms of a "macho" society that is in love with exaggerated memories of its "wild west." Like the Jews who awaited the Messiah, many today see their destiny best fulfilled by the strength of arms. This is admittedly selfish but is justified by the hope that the power will be used for righteous causes. True, few would presume the United States to always be righteous, but in a world without absolute standards it is often deemed necessary to choose that which is the lesser evil.

Yet there exists today a minority that believes the interests neither of Christ's church nor of their country lie in dependence upon armaments. These Christian pacifists believe big armies create fear and oppression, causing the victims to develop a disdain for Christ if He is presented as an aspect of American culture and under the protection of American arms. One of many adverse results is that oppressive armies thus become an impediment to evangelism.

These pacifists believe unconditional love grounded on the power of Pentecost would, if widely practiced, end much oppression and injustice and result in an open door to the evangelization of those who resist force but would welcome love. They model after the growth of the early church and that of the historic peace churches. The seventeenth century Quakers, for example, taught and practiced an uncompromised New Testament ethic and grew to somewhere between 30,000 and 60,000 in ten years.[1]

Pacifism is seen to be more practical than is fighting, even if the short-term, strictly selfish results may seem negative. The pacifist dreams of what might happen if Christians were willing to spend as much money and as many lives in waging peace as are now squandered for armaments and war. He desires to be an activist, overcoming evil with good and substituting the weapons of spiritual warfare for those of the world. Admitting that following Christ has brought reproach, persecution, and even execution to some, he believes the true test is not the pragmatic "what works," but "what does Christ want me to do?" Love for God and neighbor is always the key.

The pacifist may not hate war more than the non-pacifist; nor, perhaps, is he more "loving." Yet his love is unconditional—he attempts to replace the moral relativism of the just war with absolute obedience to God. All other considerations must be secondary.

Many questions follow this profound, life-changing pronouncement. For example, what degree of nonviolent resistance should I use to restrain evil? What if the aggressor invades? How can I best avail myself of the weapons of spiritual warfare to combat evil? What adjustments can I make in my lifestyle that will reduce the possibility that the seeds of war will be nourished by the way I live?

These are difficult questions. No person can be totally consistent. All are probably open to some criticism.

---

[1] William C. Braithwaite, *The Beginnings of Quakerism* (London: Macmillan and Co., Limited, 1912), p. 512 and 512n.

But again, all questions, no matter how difficult, must be held as subsidiary to the one principal decision—that Christ's disciples must renounce the option to kill people.

The questions are even more difficult for the non-pacifistic Christian, who must try to reconcile his philosophy with Christ's teachings, and who is placed in the uncomfortably ambiguous position of arguing for the use of evil means to combat evil—a method that has proven again and again to reap the whirlwind of hatred, oppression, and injustice.

A natural result of a total Christian experience is the kind of unconditional love that makes the believer a pacifist. To love unconditionally is to be a pacifist and to be a pacifist is to love unconditionally. Moving toward biblical pacifism is a sometimes painful, often slow, always Christ-guided growth away from prejudice and hatred into the truth that Christ promised would set His people free.

This chart suggests the teaching of various Christians through church history on the subject of violence.

	Biblical Pacifism Position	Just War Position	Holy War (Crusade) Position
✝	Christ, Early Church		
		Augustine	
A.D. 500			
A.D. 1000	Monks		Crusading Church
	St. Francis		
A.D. 1500		Luther, Calvin	
	Anabaptists, Quakers		Puritans
A.D. 2000	"New Evangelicals"	"Nuclear Pacifists"	"Neo-Just War" Advocates	Anti-Communist Crusaders

What Jesus Said Could Happen to His Disciples

Struck physically (Matthew 5:39)

Persecuted (Matthew 5:44; John 15:20)

Arrested (Mark 13:11)

Flogged (Mark 13:9)

Hated (Mark 13:13; John 15:19; Matthew 10:22-23; Luke 6:22; Luke 21:17)

Delivered up to death by family members (Mark 13:12)

Cursed (Luke 6:28)

Mistreated (Luke 6:28)

Ostracized (Luke 6:22)

Insulted (Luke 6:22)

Killed (Matthew 10:28; Luke 21:16)

Tribulation (John 16:33)

Thrown into prisons (Luke 21:12)

Delivered up to the synagogues to be judged (Luke 21:12)

Betrayed by family (Luke 21:16)

Killed by family (Luke 21:16)

How Jesus Says to Respond

Turn the other cheek (Matthew 5:39; Luke 6:29).

Pray when persecuted (Matthew 5:44; Luke 6:27).

Love our enemies (Matthew 5:44; Luke 6:27).

Forgive (Matthew 18:21-22; Mark 11:25).

Do not be anxious (Mark 13:11).

Endure to the end (Mark 13:13).

Do good to those who hate us (Luke 6:27).

Bless those who curse us (Luke 6:28).

Pray for those who mistreat us (Luke 6:28).

Remember that if they persecuted Jesus they will persecute us (John 15:20).

Consider ourselves blessed when we are hated, ostracized, insulted and slandered as being evil for the sake of Jesus (Luke 6:22).

Be glad when we are treated as the persecuted prophets before us (Luke 6:23).

Leap for joy when we are treated as the persecuted prophets before us (Luke 6:23).

Flee persecution (Matthew 10:23).

Do not fear those who can kill the body (Matthew 10:28).

Do not let our hearts be troubled (John 14:27).

Do not let our hearts be fearful (John 14:27).

Take courage (John 16:33).

Do not prepare to defend ourselves (Luke 21:12-14).

What the Apostles Said Could Happen to Believers

Be harshly treated (1 Peter 2:20)

Suffer (1 Peter 2:21, 23)

Be reviled (1 Peter 2:23)

Have evil done to us (1 Peter 3:9; 1 Thessalonians 5:15; 2 Timothy 4:18)

Be slandered (1 Peter 3:16)

Be hated (1 John 3:13)

Suffer tribulation (Romans 12:12)

Be persecuted (Romans 12:14; 2 Corinthians 4:9)

Have enemies (Romans 12:20)

Be afflicted in every way (2 Corinthians 4:8)

Be struck down (2 Corinthians 4:9)

How the Apostles Said to Respond

Patiently endure unjust suffering (1 Peter 2:20).

Follow Christ's example (1 Peter 2:21-23).

> No deceit in His mouth.

> Did not revile.

> Uttered no threats.

Do not repay evil for evil (1 Peter 3:9).

Do not repay insult for insult (1 Peter 3:9).

Give a blessing to someone who has insulted you (1 Peter 3:9).

Refrain from speaking guile (1 Peter 3:10).

Seek peace and pursue it (1 Peter 3:11).

Turn away from evil (1 Peter 3:11).

Use prayer (1 Peter 3:12).

Do not be troubled (1 Peter 3:13).

Do not fear intimidation (1 Peter 3:14).

Consider ourselves blessed when persecuted for righteousness sake (1 Peter 3:14).

Sanctify Christ as Lord in our hearts (1 Peter 3:15).

Keep a good conscience (1 Peter 3:16).

Be slow to anger (James 1:19).

Realize that our anger will not achieve the righteousness of God (James 1:20).

Be patient with all men (1 Thessalonians 5:14).

Do not marvel if the world hates us (1 John 3:13).

Do not hate our brother (1 John 3:15; 1 John 2:9, 11).

Lay down our lives for our brethren (1 John 3:16).

Love without hypocrisy (Romans 12:9).

Abhor what is evil (Romans 12:9).

Cleave to what is good (Romans 12:9).

Be devoted to one another in brotherly love (Romans 12:10).

Persevere in tribulation (Romans 12:12).

Be fervent in spirit (Romans 12:11).

Do not lag behind in diligence (Romans 12:11).

Rejoice in hope (Romans 12:12).

Be devoted to prayer (Romans 12:12).

Practice hospitality (Romans 12:13).

Bless those who persecute us (Romans 12:14).

Do not curse (Romans 12:14).

Do not be haughty (Romans 12:16).

Never take revenge (Romans 12:19).

Feed your enemy and give him drink (Romans 12:20).

Be not overcome with evil, overcome evil with good (Romans 12:21).

The Response of the Apostles to Persecution as Found in the Book of Acts

Acts, Chapter 4

Type of Persecution

John and Peter arrested (v. 3), brought before the council (v. 7), and threatened (v. 21).

Cause of Persecution

The priests, the captain of the temple guard, and the Sadducees were upset that Peter and John were teaching and proclaiming about Jesus and His resurrection from the dead (vv. 1-2).

Apostles' Response to Persecution

When commanded by the Sanhedrin not to speak or teach about Jesus, Peter and John reply: "Whether it is right in the sight of God to give heed to you rather than to God, you be the judge; for we cannot stop speaking what we have seen and heard." (vv. 18-20 NASB)

After being threatened more, and after being released, Peter and John return to their companions and pray in one accord to God that he might take note of the threats and allow them to continue to speak His word with full confidence (vv. 24-30).

Acts 5:1-25

Type of Persecution

Peter and some of the apostles are arrested by the high priest and his associates (vv. 17-18).

Cause of Persecution

High priest and his associates were filled with jealousy over the healing Peter and the apostles were accomplishing (vv. 16-17).

Apostles' Response to Persecution

While they were in jail an angel of the Lord frees them, telling them to go and speak to the people in the Temple about Christ (vv. 19-20).

The apostles follow the angel's instructions (v. 25).

Acts 5:26-42

Type of Persecution

Peter and apostles are arrested again and brought before the council (vv. 26-27).

They are flogged, ordered not to speak again in the name of Jesus, and then released (v. 40).

Cause of Persecution

Council upset that apostles have continued to proclaim Christ despite a previous warning (v. 28).

Apostles' Response to Persecution

When told to stop speaking about Christ apostles respond: "We must obey God rather than men." (v. 29)

After being flogged they rejoice that they had been considered worthy to suffer shame for Jesus' name (vv. 40-41).

Continue to teach and preach about Jesus (v. 42).

Acts 6-7

Type of Persecution

Stephen dragged before Council (6:12).

Stephen stoned to death (7:58-59).

Cause of Persecution

Stephen had upset some Jews because of his witness about Christ (6:8-10).

They bring a false witness against him (6:13-14).

Apostles' Response to Persecution

When brought before the Council Stephen witnesses to them about Christ (7:1-53).

While being stoned cries out in a loud voice; "Lord, do not hold this sin against them!" (7:60)

Acts 12

Type of Persecution

Some in church mistreated (v. 1).

James murdered (v. 2).

Peter arrested, put in prison, and bound with chains
(vv. 3-6).

Cause of Persecution

Led by Herod, probably instigated by the Jews (vv. 1-3),
most likely because of the insistence of the apostles to
preach about Jesus.

Apostles' Response to Persecution

An angel frees Peter (vv. 7-11).

Peter goes to the house of Mary, mother of John Mark, and
reports to the people there what had happened; he
then departs (vv. 12-17).

Acts 13

Type of Persecution

Paul and Barnabas are driven away by the leading Jewish
men and women (v. 50).

Cause of Persecution

Jews were filled with jealousy (v. 45).

Apostles' Response to Persecution

Shook off the dust of their feet in protest and left (v. 51).

Continually filled with joy and the Holy Spirit (v. 52).

Acts 14

Type of Persecution

Paul is stoned, dragged out of the city, and left for dead
(v. 19).

Cause of Persecution

Paul and Barnabas irritated the Jews by witnessing to the Greeks about Jesus and by healing a lame man (vv. 8-19).

Apostles' Response to Persecution

Disciples stand around Paul after he has been left for dead. He then gets up and enters the city again (v. 20).

Paul encourages disciples to continue in the faith saying: "Through many tribulations we must enter the kingdom of God." (v. 22)

Acts 16:12-29

Type of Persecution

Paul and Silas are dragged before the authorities (v. 19).

They have their robes torn off and are beaten with rods (v. 22).

They are then thrown into prison and have their feet fastened in stocks (vv. 23-24).

Cause of Persecution

Paul had commanded a spirit of divination to come out of a slave girl, resulting in a loss of income to her owners (vv. 16-19).

Apostles' Response to Persecution

With other prisoners listening, Paul and Silas pray and sing hymns of praise to God (v. 25).

Are freed by an earthquake (v. 26).

Paul prevents the jailer (who thought they had escaped) from committing suicide (vv. 27-28).

Paul leads the jailer and his household to Christianity (vv. 30-34).

Acts 21-26

Type of Persecution

Paul dragged out of the Temple (21:30)

Arrested by the Romans for his own protection and held in chains (21:31-33).

Held prisoner for a long period of time (21:31 through end of chapter 26).

Cause of Persecution

Jews upset over the teachings of Paul and because they thought he had brought Gentiles into the Temple (21:28).

Apostles' Response to Persecution

When under Roman authority Paul calls upon his rights as a Roman citizen (22:25-28; 25:11).

Continually witnessed about Christ.

Does Jesus Consider Peacemaking Important?

"But I say to you, Love your enemies and pray for those who persecute you, so that you may be sons of your Father who is in heaven...." Matthew 5:44-45 (Luke 6:27, 35)

"If you love those who love you, what credit is that to you? For even sinners love those who love them. And if you do good to those who do good to you, what credit is that to you? For even sinners do the same." Luke 6:32-33 (Matthew 5:46-47)

"You have heard that it was said to the men of old, 'You shall not kill; and whoever kills shall be liable to judgment.' But I say to you that every one who is angry with his brother shall be liable to judgment; whoever insults his brother shall be liable to the council, and whoever says 'You fool!' shall be liable to the hell of fire." Matthew 5:21-22

"Judge not, and you will not be judged; condemn not, and you will not be condemned; forgive, and you will be forgiven...." Luke 6:37 (Matthew 7:1-2)

"For if you forgive men their trespasses, your heavenly Father also will forgive you; but if you do not forgive men their trespasses, neither will your Father forgive your trespasses." Matthew 6:14-15 (Matthew 18:35; Mark 11:25)

"Therefore you have no excuse, O man, whoever you are, when you judge another; for in passing judgment upon him you condemn yourself, because you, the judge, are doing the very same things. We know that the judgment of God rightly falls upon those who do such things. Do you suppose, O man, that when you judge those who

51

do such things and yet do them yourself, you will escape the judgment of God?" Romans 2:1-3

"Then Jesus said to him, 'Put your sword back into its place; for all who take the sword will perish by the sword.'" Matthew 26:52 (Revelation 13:10)

"Now the works of the flesh are plain: immorality, impurity, licentiousness, idolatry, sorcery, enmity, strife, jealousy, anger, selfishness, dissension, party spirit, envy, drunkenness, carousing, and the like. I warn you, as I warned you before, that those who do such things shall not inherit the kingdom of God." Galatians 5:19-21 (Romans 1:28-32; 13:13; 1 Corinthians 3:3; 2 Corinthians 12:20; Ephesians 4:31; Philippians 2:3; Colossians 3:8; 1 Timothy 6:3-5; 2 Timothy 2:23-26; Titus 3:2-3; James 3:14-16)

"He who says he is in the light and hates his brother is in the darkness still. He who loves his brother abides in the light, and in it there is no cause for stumbling. But he who hates his brother is in the darkness and walks in the darkness, and does not know where he is going, because the darkness has blinded his eyes." 1 John 2:9-11

"By this it may be seen who are the children of God, and who are the children of the devil: whoever does not do right is not of God, nor he who does not love his brother. For this is the message which you have heard from the beginning, that we should love one another." 1 John 3:10-11

"We know that we have passed out of death into life, because we love the brethren. He who does not love remains in death. Any one who hates his brother is a murderer, and you know that no murderer has eternal life abiding in him." 1 John 3:14-15

"If anyone says, 'I love God,' and hates his brother, he is a liar; for he who does not love his brother whom he has seen, cannot love God whom he has not seen." 1 John 4:20

Christ's Kingdom
Is Not of This World

"And the devil took him up, and showed him all the kingdoms of the world in a moment of time, and said to him, 'To you I will give all this authority and their glory; for it has been delivered to me; and I give it to whom I will. If you, then, will worship me, it shall all be yours.'" Luke 4:5-7 (Matthew 4:8-9)

"We know that we are of God, and the whole world is in the power of the evil one." 1 John 5:19

"...for the ruler of this world is coming. He has no power over me...." John 14:30

"Yet among the mature we do impart wisdom, although it is not a wisdom of this age or of the rulers of this age, who are doomed to pass away." 1 Corinthians 2:6

"...For the form of this world is passing away." 1 Corinthians 7:31

"For we brought nothing into the world, and we cannot take anything out of the world." 1 Timothy 6:7

"Do not be mismated with unbelievers. For what partnership have righteousness and iniquity? Or what fellowship has light with darkness? What accord has Christ with Belial? Or what has a believer in common with an unbeliever? What agreement has the temple of God with idols? For we are the temple of the living God; as God said, 'I will live in them and move among them, and I will be their God, and they shall be my people. Therefore come out from them, and be separate from them, says the Lord, and touch nothing unclean; then I will welcome you, and I will be a father to you, and you shall be my sons and daughters, says the Lord Almighty.'" 2 Corinthians 6:14-18

"Unfaithful creatures! Do you not know that friendship with the world is enmity with God? Therefore whoever wishes to be a friend of the world makes himself an enemy of God." James 4:4

"Do not love the world or the things in the world. If any one loves the world, love for the Father is not in him. For all that is in the world, the lust of the flesh and the lust of the eyes and the pride of life, is not of the Father but is of the world. And the world passes away, and the lust of it; but he who does the will of God abides for ever." 1 John 2:15-17

"Then Jesus told his disciples, 'If any man would come after me, let him deny himself and take up his cross and follow me. For whoever would save his life will lose it, and whoever loses his life for my sake will find it. For what will it profit a man, if he gains the whole world and forfeits his life? Or what shall a man give in return for his life? For the Son of man is to come with his angels in the glory of his Father, and then he will repay every man for what he has done.'" Matthew 16:24-28 (Mark 8:36; Luke 9:25; John 12:25)

"Jesus answered, 'My kingdom is not of this world. If My kingdom were of this world, then My servants would be fighting, that I might not be delivered up to the Jews; but as it is My kingdom is not of this realm.'" John 18:36 NASB

"For we are not contending against flesh and blood, but against the principalities, against the powers, against the world rulers of this present darkness, against the spiritual hosts of wickedness in the heavenly places." Ephesians 6:12

"Do not be conformed to this world but be transformed by the renewal of your mind, that you may prove what is the will of God, what is good and acceptable and perfect." Romans 12:2

"Blessed are the poor in spirit, for theirs is the kingdom of heaven.

"Blessed are those who hunger and thirst for righteousness, for they shall be satisfied.

"Blessed are the merciful, for they shall obtain mercy.

"Blessed are the pure in heart, for they shall see God.

"Blessed are the peacemakers, for they shall be called sons of God." Matthew 5:3-9

See also Matthew 13:22; Mark 4:19; Luke 12:29-31; John 1:10; 8:23; 12:31; 15:19; 16:8-11; 17:14-18; 1 Corinthians 11:32; 2 Corinthians 4:4; Titus 2:11-12; James 1:27; 2 Peter 1:4; 2:20; Revelation 12:9.

STUDY & TEACHING AIDS

Does Violence in the Old Testament Mean We Can Be Violent?

The Old Testament is the record of creation and fall; the New Testament is the story of redemption and reconciliation through the power of Christ's atonement. Both Old and New are essential to an understanding of the message of salvation.

Sin is the problem; Christ is the solution. To live by the Old Testament norm is to accept second best, since Christ came to fulfill, to perfect the old law. While man's sin in the garden of Eden set the pattern for selfish and violent behavior, Christ's teaching, example, and death introduced the power to live in His love.

"You have heard that it was said, 'An eye for an eye and a tooth for a tooth.' But I say to you...." (Matthew 5:38-39) "You have heard that it was said, 'You shall love your neighbor and hate your enemy.' But I say to you...." (Matthew 5:43-44) Jesus brought a new standard. It is not possible to accept His teachings and still live with vindictive attitudes. It just cannot be done. We have to choose one or the other.

Obedience to God's Commandments Is the Issue
The devastating results of the fall could never be overturned by anything less than God sending His Son as Redeemer. Nevertheless, from time to time God did offer the children of Israel a foretaste of the kingdom age.

For example, in the covenant He established with them at Mt. Sinai He promised that if they would obey Him He would "be an enemy to your enemies" and use His angel and hornets as their military (Exodus 23:22-28). He

57

also directed them to establish jubilee—a system of equitable, just use of property (Leviticus 25).

But the Israelites sinned. The sword replaced the angel and injustice won out over jubilee. In their disobedience they left a legacy of bloodshed. Still, God provided a unique protection of the nation through which He had chosen to bring the Messiah into the world. His primary will had been frustrated by sin in the Garden of Eden; His secondary will had been frustrated by their disobedience in refusing to enter Canaan. Now He offered a third alternative: the Israelites would fight their own battles and they would be successful to the extent that they obeyed Him. If they fought when God had told them not to, they met defeat (Numbers 14:39-45). When they refused to fight at God's command they were punished (Numbers 13:1-25).

Caleb and Joshua are two of the shining Old Testament examples of obedience to God. Following His commands (Numbers 14:7-9) was more important to them than their God-given victories on the battlefields. The Lord refers to Joshua as a man in whom the Spirit dwelt (Numbers 27:18). He called Caleb a servant who had obeyed Him perfectly (Numbers 14:23-24). These men focused their lives on God and, being true servants, followed His command without hesitation, whether it led to war or to peace.

The Old Testament is full of examples of obedient men who followed God's commandments even when it did not seem to make much sense at first. God told Noah to build an ark of enormous size (Genesis 6:14-15). Noah built it. God told Abraham to use his only son, Isaac, as a human sacrifice (Genesis 22:1-14). Abraham did not hesitate to follow. Because of Abraham's faithfulness Isaac lived and God's commands continued to live within Abraham. God came to Moses, to use him as the deliverer of His people. It didn't make much sense to Moses, being slow of speech and tongue (Exodus 4:10). But he followed, and led God's people.

Noah, Abraham, and Moses had no choice but to follow God's commandments, for they were true servants of God.

Jesus gave a new commandment: "...love one another, even as I have loved you...." (John 13:34) The apostle Paul described the quality of this love when he wrote: "Love is patient and kind; love is not jealous or boastful; it is not arrogant or rude. Love does not insist on its own way; it is not irritable or resentful; it does not rejoice at wrong, but rejoices in the right. Love bears all things, believes all things, hopes all things, endures all things." (1 Corinthians 13:4-7)

Jesus went to a mountain. With Him came John, Peter, and James. As He prayed Moses and Elijah appeared. What a sight for the apostles to behold! Then came a voice from a cloud that said: "This is my Son, my Chosen; listen to him!" (Luke 9:28-35) The voice did not speak of Moses the lawgiver, or Elijah the prophet, but only of Jesus. It is to Him His followers must listen.

Christ Gives Scripture Its Consistent Application
If killing in the Old Testament legitimizes the taking of life by Christians today, it seems logical to live by all the old law. For instance: "Every one who curses his father or his mother shall be put to death." (Leviticus 20:9) God ordained this—must Christians follow it today? The Mosaic law gives clear instruction that rebellious children who will not listen to their parents must be stoned to death (Deuteronomy 21:18-21; see also Deuteronomy 13:6-11). God ordained this too. Why not follow it? What about the Old Testament practice of polygamy and concubinage? Although God did not command them, they were condoned. Does He condone them today?

Those who justify war and capital punishment by citing the Old Testament must also justify the execution of rebellious children, the offering of animal sacrifices, and a host of other Old Testament laws. But Christ died to introduce a new way—the way of love and peace. In the Old Testament it was "life for life, eye for eye, tooth for tooth, hand for hand, foot for foot." (Deuteronomy 19:21) In the New, Jesus counters with: "But I say to you, Do not resist one who is evil. But if any one strikes you on the right cheek, turn to him the other also." (Matthew 5:39) The way of peace is consistent with the teachings of Christ.

The Example of the Apostle Paul

It was as a Pharisee, well-learned in the Old Testament, that Paul persecuted Christians whom he thought were blaspheming God by proclaiming Jesus as Lord (Acts 8:3). He justified the stoning of Stephen and others by the Mosaic law he knew so well (Leviticus 24:10-16). Subsequently Paul became a Christian and recognized that it was the nonbelieving Jews rather than the Christian Jews who were actually blaspheming God. He still retained his knowledge of the Mosaic law: blasphemers must die! But instead of following that law he proclaimed the love of Christ.

It was as a Christian that Paul wrote: "But now we are discharged from the law, dead to that which held us captive, so that we serve not under the old written code but in the new life of the Spirit." (Romans 7:6) Paul the Christian versus Paul the Pharisee: both knew the Old Testament. One lived a life of peace; the other justified violence. One knew Christ, the other did not.

The 'Problem Passages' in the New Testament

Obedience to the State

Romans 13:1-7 (Titus 3:1; 1 Peter 2:13-17)

Let every person be subject to the governing authorities. For there is no authority except from God, and those that exist have been instituted by God. Therefore he who resists the authorities resists what God has appointed, and those who resist will incur judgment. For rulers are not a terror to good conduct, but to bad. Would you have no fear of him who is in authority? Then do what is good, and you will receive his approval, for he is God's servant for your good. But if you do wrong, be afraid, for he does not bear the sword in vain; he is the servant of God to execute his wrath on the wrongdoer. Therefore one must be subject, not only to avoid God's wrath but also for the sake of conscience. For the same reason you also pay taxes, for the authorities are ministers of God, attending to this very thing. Pay all of them their dues, taxes to whom taxes are due, revenue to whom revenue is due, respect to whom respect is due, honor to whom honor is due.

These Scriptures are often used to justify violence by Christians. Some reason that if the government calls them to arms they must be in subjection and follow that call. Why were these Scriptures written? What is their context and do they contain a call to war, or is it a call to peace?

Zealots were a significant revolutionary group during Jesus' lifetime. They epitomized the nationalistic Jewish fervor that desired independence from Roman rule. And they had good reason to dislike Rome. The Romans worshiped Caesar as God. In it sexual immorality was rampant. Its entertainment was cruel and inhuman. To this oppressive political state the Jews were forced to submit.

No doubt many of the early Christians were Jews who came to know Christ while still harboring negative attitudes toward the Roman state. Even one of the Twelve was a zealot. Though the Lord had changed their lives, to them the government remained the same evil institution. They were still frustrated about its control.

Paul and Peter told these Christians to be peaceful, patient, and loving subjects of the government. Do not war with the government, the apostles said. Do as it tells you, even if it seems unfair. In this they echoed Jesus' call to go the extra mile for the Roman soldier, to love their enemies, and to pray for those who persecuted them (Matthew 5:41, 44-45).

The two verses immediately before Romans 13 read: "If your enemy is hungry, feed him; if he is thirsty, give him drink...." "Do not be overcome by evil, but overcome evil with good." (Romans 12:20-21) Romans 13:8 continues: "Owe no one anything, except to love one another; for he who loves his neighbor has fulfilled the law." Titus 3:2 exhorts "to speak evil of no one, to avoid quarreling, to be gentle, and to show perfect courtesy toward all men."

Peter sums up his call to submission by declaring: "Finally, all of you, have unity of spirit, sympathy, love of the brethren, a tender heart and a humble mind. Do not return evil for evil or reviling for reviling; but on the contrary bless, for to this you have been called, that you may obtain a blessing." (1 Peter 3:8-9)

These verses are basic to an understanding of the call to subjection. They are messages of peace, not war. They require doing good even to representatives of institutions that might act unfairly.

Some teach that when Paul writes of the governing Roman authority as God's servant who "does not bear the sword in vain" he justified violence by the political state and by Christians if they became part of that state. Early church history indicates that this was a foreign thought to the Christians of the first century.

Paul writes of the Roman government as a "servant" of God only because, in spite of itself, it was serving God. The Roman government certainly had no salvation. But Paul was grateful that because of the *Pax Romana,* the peace of Rome, he was able to travel through the entire Roman empire to preach the Gospel. Though the Roman government worshiped Caesar, God used it to protect Paul from mobs and unjust punishment (Acts 16:37; 21:39; 22:25; 23:17-22; 25:10-12). Christians were thankful that the Roman state kept their cities and areas somewhat safe from criminals. The Roman government did not believe in Jesus. It participated in His crucifixion. Yet in spite of itself, the Roman government served God's purposes.

Paul and Peter told Christians to be submissive to the authorities. But they never intended their call to subjection to be interpreted as a call to blind obedience. Replacing the word *authorities* in Romans 13 with "Hitler" or any other leader's name indicates the danger of thinking the call to subjection requires blind obedience. Romans 13:1-2 could then be paraphrased—Let every person be subject to Hitler. For Hitler comes from God, and was established by God. Therefore he who resists Hitler has opposed an ordinance of God.

Christians are to be subject to the world's rulers, even the Hitlers, and be willing to go an extra mile, in love, for them. But that subjection must stop whenever the state requires behavior that would place the Christian in conflict with Christ's teachings. "We must obey God rather than men" was Peter's reply after his arrest for proclaiming Christ (Acts 5:29). That reply is expected of all Christians whenever their governments require them to act in conflict with the teachings of Christ.

Cornelius—Acts 10

A Roman centurion named Cornelius was the first Gentile to be converted to Christianity. His conversion came as the result of an amazing intercession from God. First an angel of the Lord appeared to Cornelius giving him instructions to send for Peter the apostle. At almost the same time, Peter received a vision from God that instructed him not to consider "any man common or unclean." Cornelius sent three men for Peter and the apostle returned with them. To the entourage of friends and relatives that Cornelius had gathered, Peter related how the Mosaic law prohibited a Jew from visiting with foreigners, Gentiles being included. But, he continued, the Lord, through the vision he had received, had clearly shown him that Christ's salvation was meant for all people, Jew and Gentile alike. Peter then witnessed about Jesus, and the Holy Spirit fell upon all those who had been listening.

Some wonder that since a centurion was the first Gentile Christian and there was no clear instruction for him to leave his profession, the Lord perhaps sanctions military service. This is an argument based on silence. Such arguments can be very misleading. (Not much can be learned from what the Bible does not say.)

Cornelius was a godly man before he became a Christian. But this does not mean changes were not needed in his life. Christ accepted him as he was, just as He did Saul of Tarsus. In God's plan, salvation opens the door to changed behavior. We have no record of how Cornelius's life was affected by his conversion, but we have no reason to assume he continued as a centurion. On the contrary, historical evidence from the first century would suggest that Cornelius did leave his position as centurion, as there is no record of any Christian having served with the Roman military during that time.

The importance of this passage is that both Jew and Gentile could be saved and that we must "not call any man common or unclean." That includes Nazis, Communists, Klan members—everyone. Is it possible to use this passage to justify violence against those whom the Lord says are not common and unclean? If so, does not the Christian revert back to the mentality that separated the Jews and the Gentiles? God calls to a higher standard: to love one's neighbor as oneself. This includes loving one's enemies in the hope that by that example they may come to share in salvation.

Peter, by trusting the Spirit, went in love to a centurion's home and led him to the Lord. He did not go there to condemn nor to endorse the centurion's life in the army. Peter's example of trust and love is a model for all Christians.

"I Came Not to Bring Peace, but a Sword . . . ." (Matthew 10:34-39)

Do not think that I have come to bring peace on earth; I have not come to bring peace, but a sword. For I have come to set a man against his father, and a daughter against her mother, and a daughter-in-law against her mother-in-law; and a man's foes will be those of his own household. He who loves father or mother more than me is not worthy of me; and he who loves son or daughter more than me is not worthy of me; and he who does not take his cross and follow me is not worthy of me. He who finds his life will lose it, and he who loses his life for my sake will find it.

This passage is sometimes used to imply that Christ speaks of the sword in a literal sense and that we too may use it.

Jesus does not bring peace to non-Christians. He brings peace to the Christian who has surrendered his will to Him (John 14:27). In this passage He uses the word *sword* figuratively, referring to the unrest a Jewish family would have when one of its members became a Christian. Jesus told His early listeners that in choosing Him they might be betrayed, delivered up to death, or even killed by their family members (Luke 21:16; also see Luke 12:51-53).

Jesus implies that Christians might lose their lives as a result of a decision to follow Him (Matthew 10:39). Nowhere does this passage imply that Christians should use weapons in taking another's life. It does not support violence by the Christian. Instead Jesus stated that the will of the Lord is more important even than the family. Anyone who seeks to protect his family by taking life chooses the family and its temporal safety over the teachings of Jesus (see Luke 14:26-27).

Go and Buy a Sword (Luke 22:36-38)

"...let him who has no sword sell his mantle and buy one. For I tell you that this scripture must be fulfilled in me, 'And he was reckoned with transgressors'; for what is written about me has its fulfillment." And they said, "Look, Lord, here are two swords." And He said to them, "It is enough."

This puzzling passage seems to suggest that Christ was arming for His defense against impending arrest. It would follow that Christians today should arm themselves against evil persons. But Christ never intended for the disciples to use the swords violently. By carrying swords Jesus' band would have the appearance of criminals. This Jesus desired in order that He might be reckoned with transgressors, a despised, rejected outlaw (Isaiah 53:12).

It should be noted that when the disciples stated that they had two swords, Jesus told them that would be enough. He surely would have ordered more if He had planned for them to be used as weapons.

When Jesus was about to be arrested the disciples asked: "Lord, shall we strike with the sword?" Immediately Peter, in defense of his Lord, struck a man and cut off his ear. Jesus quickly responded: "No more of this!" He then healed the man who had come to arrest Him (Luke 22:49-51), and warned His disciples that those who killed with the sword would die by it (Matthew 26:52).

Jesus' example, teaching, and reproof of Peter make it clear He never intended His disciples to use swords for violence. The record of their subsequent lives proved they learned this lesson well.

Jesus and the Whip (John 2:13-16)

The Passover of the Jews was at hand, and Jesus went up to Jerusalem. In the temple he found those who were selling oxen and sheep and pigeons, and the money-changers at their business. And making a whip of cords, he drove them all, with the sheep and oxen, out of the temple; and he poured out the coins of the money-changers and overturned their tables. And he told those who sold the pigeons, "Take these things away; you shall not make my Father's house a house of trade."

Some believe that when Jesus used a whip of cords in ridding the Temple of the money-changers and sacrifice-sellers, He by example sanctioned violence by His followers. No one was in mortal danger, of course, nor is there any indication that Jesus actually struck anyone with the cords.

But even if Jesus had used the whip it would not sanction violence by His believers. "Let him who is without sin among you be the first to throw a stone at her," was Jesus' reply to the Jews who sought to have a woman stoned for being caught in the act of adultery (John 8:7). Jesus was the only sinless person there. He was the only one who had a right to condemn. He was also the only one who had a right to cleanse the Temple in the manner He did.

Christ's Example

"...Christ also suffered for you, leaving you an example, that you should follow in his steps. He committed no sin; no guile was found on his lips. When he was reviled, he did not revile in return; when he suffered, he did not threaten; but he trusted to him who judges justly. He himself bore our sins in his body on the tree, that we might die to sin and live to righteousness." (1 Peter 2:21-24)

"Consider him who endured from sinners such hostility against himself...." (Hebrews 12:3)

"Although he was a Son, he learned obedience through what he suffered." (Hebrews 5:8)

"Christ redeemed us from the curse of the law, having become a curse for us—for it is written, 'Cursed be every one who hangs on a tree.'" (Galatians 3:13)

"For you know the grace of our Lord Jesus Christ, that though he was rich, yet for your sake he became poor, so that by his poverty you might become rich." (2 Corinthians 8:9)

"...the Son of man came not to be served but to serve, and to give his life as a ransom for many." (Matthew 20:28)

"Take my yoke upon you, and learn from me; for I am gentle and lowly in heart, and you will find rest for your souls." (Matthew 11:29)

"Have this mind among yourselves, which you have in Christ Jesus, who, though he was in the form of God, did not count equality with God a thing to be grasped, but emptied himself, taking the form of a servant, being born in the likeness of men. And being found in human form he humbled himself and became obedient unto death, even death on a cross." (Philippians 2:5-8)

"He was oppressed, and he was afflicted, yet he opened not his mouth; like a lamb that is led to the slaughter, and like a sheep that before its shearers is dumb, so he opened not his mouth. By oppression and judgment he was taken away...And they made his grave with the wicked...although he had done no violence, and there was no deceit in his mouth." (Isaiah 53:7-9)

Is It Important
to Teach Peacemaking?

Scripture often indicates that the peace stand
is not optional, but must be obeyed
if we are to be in God's will.

"I say to you, Love your enemies and pray for those who persecute you, so that you may be sons of your Father who is in heaven...." (Matthew 5:44-45; also see Luke 6:27, 35)

"If you love those who love you, what credit is that to you? For even sinners love those who love them. And if you do good to those who do good to you, what credit is that to you? For even sinners do the same." (Luke 6:32-33; also see Matthew 5:46-47)

"You have heard that it was said to the men of old, 'You shall not kill; and whoever kills shall be liable to judgment.' But I say to you that every one who is angry with his brother shall be liable to judgment; whoever insults his brother shall be liable to the council, and whoever says, 'You fool!' shall be liable to the hell of fire." (Matthew 5:21-22)

"Judge not, and you will not be judged; condemn not, and you will not be condemned; forgive, and you will be forgiven...." (Luke 6:37; also see Matthew 7:1-2)

"For if you forgive men their trespasses, your heavenly Father also will forgive you; but if you do not forgive men their trespasses, neither will your Father forgive your trespasses." (Matthew 6:14-15; also see Matthew 18:35; Mark 11:25)

"Therefore you have no excuse, O man, whoever you are, when you judge another; for in passing judgment

71

upon him you condemn yourself, because you, the judge, are doing the very same things. We know that the judgment of God rightly falls upon those who do such things. Do you suppose, O man, that when you judge those who do such things and yet do them yourself, you will escape the judgment of God?" (Romans 2:1-3)

"Now the works of the flesh are plain: fornication [immorality], impurity, licentiousness, idolatry, sorcery, enmity, strife, jealousy, anger, selfishness, dissension, party spirit, envy, drunkenness, carousing, and the like. I warn you, as I warned you before, that those who do such things shall not inherit the kingdom of God." (Galatians 5:19-21; also see Romans 1:28-32; Romans 13:13; 1 Corinthians 3:3; 2 Corinthians 12:20; Ephesians 4:31; Philippians 2:3; Colossians 3:8; 1 Timothy 6:4; 2 Timothy 2:23-26; Titus 3:2-3; James 3:14-16)

"He who says he is in the light and hates his brother is in the darkness still. He who loves his brother abides in the light, and in it there is no cause for stumbling. But he who hates his brother is in the darkness and walks in the darkness, and does not know where he is going, because the darkness has blinded his eyes." (1 John 2:9-11)

"By this it may be seen who are the children of God, and who are the children of the devil: whoever does not do right is not of God, nor he who does not love his brother. For this is the message which you have heard from the beginning, that we should love one another...." (1 John 3:10-11)

"We know that we have passed out of death into life, because we love the brethren. He who does not love remains [abides] in death. Any one who hates his brother is a murderer, and you know that no murderer has eternal life abiding in him." (1 John 3:14-15)

"If any one says 'I love God,' and hates his brother, he is a liar; for he who does not love his brother whom he has seen, cannot love God whom he has not seen. And this commandment we have from him, that he who loves God should love his brother also." (1 John 4:20-21)

"If I speak in the tongues of men and of angels, but have not love, I am a noisy gong or a clanging cymbal. And if I have prophetic powers, and understand all mysteries and all knowledge, and if I have all faith, so as to remove mountains, but have not love, I am nothing. If I give away all I have, and if I deliver my body to be burned, but have not love, I gain nothing." (1 Corinthians 13:1-3)

"...the anger of man does not work the righteousness of God." (James 1:20)

"...where jealousy and selfish ambition exist, there will be disorder and every vile practice. But the wisdom from above is first pure, then peaceable, gentle...." (James 3:16-17)

"Then Jesus said to him, 'Put your sword back into its place; for all who take the sword will perish by the sword.'" (Matthew 26:52; see also Revelation 13:10)

The Armor of God

God does not leave the
nonviolent Christian powerless.
To him He gives not the armor of the world
but that from another source.
These Scriptures tell of that armor.

"The night is far gone, the day is at hand. Let us then cast off the works of darkness and put on the armor of light." (Romans 13:12)

"For though we live in the world we are not carrying on a worldly war, for the weapons of our warfare are not worldly but have divine power to destroy strongholds." (2 Corinthians 10:3-4)

"Put on the whole armor of God, that you may be able to stand against the wiles of the devil. For we are not contending against flesh and blood, but against the principalities, against the powers, against the world rulers of this present darkness, against the spiritual hosts of wickedness in the heavenly places. Therefore take the whole armor of God, that you may be able to withstand in the evil day, and having done all, to stand. Stand therefore, having girded your loins with truth, and having put on the breastplate of righteousness, and having shod your feet with the equipment of the gospel of peace; above all [besides all these] taking the shield of faith, with which you can quench all the flaming darts of the evil one. And take the helmet of salvation, and the sword of the Spirit, which is the word of God." (Ephesians 6:11-17)

"But, since we belong to the day, let us be sober, and put on the breastplate of faith and love, and for a helmet the hope of salvation. For God has not destined us for wrath, but to obtain salvation through our Lord Jesus Christ, who died for us so that whether we wake or sleep we might live with him." (1 Thessalonians 5:8-10)

Suggestions for Further Study

Abrams, Ray H., *Preachers Present Arms: The Role of the American Churches and Clergy in World Wars I and II with Some Observations on the War in Vietnam* (Scottdale, Pa.: Herald Press) 1969. Explains ways in which world war was turned into holy war and given the sanction of religion.

Aukerman, Dale, *Darkening Valley: A Biblical Perspective of Nuclear War* (New York: Seabury Press) 1981, 282 pp. A powerful work that describes the shape of our theological existence today.

Bainton, Roland H., *Christian Attitudes Toward War and Peace* (Nashville: Abingdon), 1960, 299 pp. Considered the classic on the church's historical stand relative to violence.

Clouse, Robert G., *The Cross and the Flag* (Carol Stream, Ill.: Creation House) 1972, 238 pp. An excellent set of essays on church/state issues.

_____, ed., *War: Four Christian Views* (Downers Grove: Inter Varsity Press) 1981. Essays of two pacifists and two who accept the just war doctrine with responses.

Ferguson, John, *The Politics of Love: The New Testament and Nonviolent Revolution* (Nyack, N.Y.: Fellowship Publications, 1979), 122 pp. Takes a hard look into some of the passages often used as arguments for war, and examines the early church.

Hadley, Norval, ed., *New Call to Peacemaking: A Challenge to All Friends* (Plainfield, Ind.: Friends World Committee for Consultation), 1976, 80 pp. The original booklet of the New Call to Peacemaking, including important chapters on the need for a biblical witness and the "just war" position of much of the church.

Holmes, Arthur, ed., *War and Christian Ethics* (Grand Rapids: Baker Book House) 1975, 353 pp. An excellent history of the Christian church's various positions on war.

Hornus, Jean Michael, *It Is Not Lawful for Me to Fight* (Scottdale, Pa.; Herald Press) 1980, 384 pp. Early Christian attitudes toward war, violence and the state and their relevance for our own violent age.

Kehler, Larry, *The Rule of the Lamb: A Study Guide on Civil Responsibility* (Newton, Kans.: Faith and Life Press), 1978, 68 pp. A study of the Christian's responsibility to his government and to Christ.

Lind, Millard, *Yahweh Is a Warrior* (Scottdale, Pa.: Herald Press) 1980, 248 pp. The theology of warfare in ancient Israel.

McSorley, Richard, *New Testament Basis of Peacemaking* (Washington, D.C.: Center for Peace Studies), 1979, 167 pp. A rich source of information about where Christ and the early Church stood on the subject of peacemaking.

Macy, Howard R., *The Shalom of God* (Richmond, Ind.: Friends United Press) 1979, 36 pp. Peace in the Old and New Testaments.

Mills, Paul M., *The Bible and War* (Newberg: Barclay Press) 1968, 24 pp. An excellent brief statement of what the Bible says about war.

Shelly, Maynard, *New Call for Peacemakers* (Newton, Kans.: Faith and Life Press), 1979, 109 pp. An excellent study guide that relates biblical teaching to the realities and needs of the world today.

Sider, Ronald J., *Christ and Violence* (Scottdale, Pa.: Herald Press) 1979, 108 pp. An important collection of lecture/sermons first given at the national New Call to Peacemaking conference in 1978.

Sider, Ronald J. and Taylor, Richard K., *Nuclear Holocaust and Christian Hope* (Downers Grove: Inter Varsity Press) 1982, 492 pp. An important statement of the opportunities before Christians today.

Sine, Tom, *The Mustard Seed Conspiracy* (Waco, Texas: Word Books) 1981. A challenge to create a future based on Kingdom principles.

Wallis, Jim, *The Call to Conversion: The Gospel for These Times* (New York: Harper and Row) 1983, 208 pp. A profound statement of what it means to be a Christian today.

_____, ed., *Waging Peace: A Handbook for the Struggle Against Nuclear Arms* (New York: Harper and Row) 1982, 304 pp. An excellent source for Christians who want to make a difference.

Wells, Ronald G., ed., *Wars in America: Christian Views* (Grand Rapids: Eerdmans) 1982. Essays on America's wars, most by just war advocates, and most concluding that few if any of the wars were justifiable by Christian standards. Ralph Beebe is the author of the essay on the War of 1812.

Yoder, John H., *Nevertheless: The Varieties and Shortcomings of Religious Pacifism* (Scottdale: Herald Press) 1971, 133 pp. Classifies and describes about 15 pacifist positions.

_____, *The Original Revolution: Essays on Christian Pacifism* (Scottdale: Herald Press) 1971, 182 pp. Relates biblical pacifism to other Christian doctrines.

_____, *The Politics of Jesus* (Grand Rapids: Eerdmans) 1972, 260 pp. An important statement of what the Christian community was meant to be.